Level 2

# *The Church Musician*

*by*
David Carr Glover
*and*
Earl Ricker

**FDL 00550**

©1972 BELWIN-MILLS PUBLISHING CORP.
All Rights Administered by WARNER BROS. PUBLICATIONS U.S. INC.
All Rights Reserved including Public Performance for Profit

# Foreword

This religious repertoire book is designed to follow logically The Church Musician — Level I. It can be used with the Piano Student — Level II of the David Carr Glover Piano Library to reinforce the fundamentals of piano study through the use of traditional and new religious music. It may be introduced at any time. Should the student not complete this book before beginning Level III of the Piano Library, the materials are so designed to carry over into the first part of this level.

This book can also be used as a Level II Method Book as it presents a concise step by step approach to the fundamentals of piano study through the use of religious music. When used this way, the following materials from the David Carr Glover Piano Library — Level II are recommended for a well-rounded program. They are:

The Piano Repertoire, Piano Duets, Write and Play Major Scales books as well as all piano solos for this level are also recommended for further reinforcement and enjoyment. They can be presented at the discretion of the teacher.

# Contents

4

Rev. Charles Wesley, 1707 - 1788, was born in Epworth, England. His father was a rector in the Church of England. He was educated at Westminster school and later attended Oxford where he organized a group of students called the Oxford Methodists. He is one of the greatest hymn writers of all time, having written more than 6,500 hymns. This is one of his best-loved.

# Jesus Lover Of My Soul

CHARLES WESLEY

SIMON B. MARSH

**TEACHER:**

On page 8 all three notes of the I and V7 chords are introduced. You may, however, prefer to present them at this time. It is suggested that the student draw in the missing note for each chord.

FDL 550

©1972 BELWIN-MILLS PUBLISHING CORP.
All Rights Administered by WARNER BROS. PUBLICATIONS U.S. INC.
All Rights Reserved including Public Performance for Profit

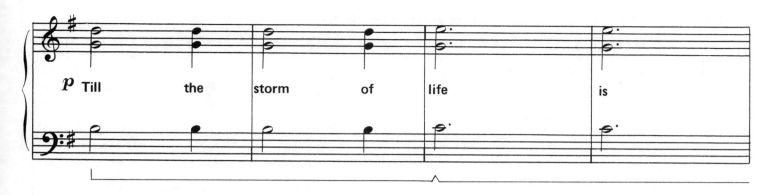

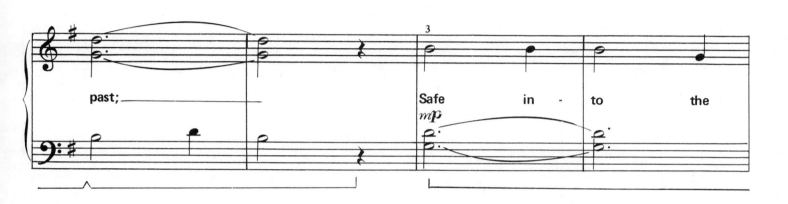

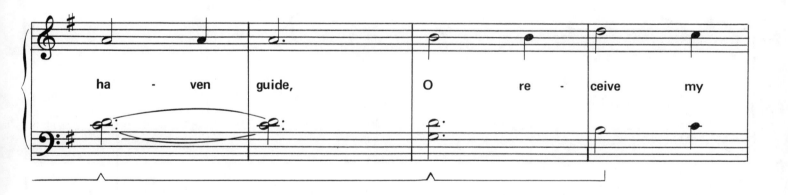

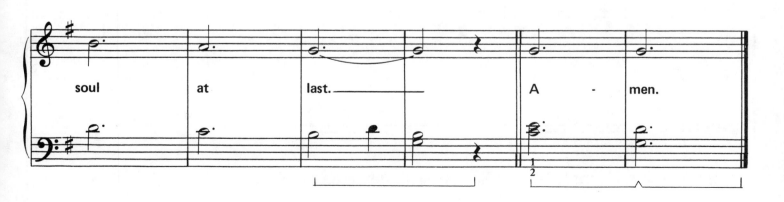

FDL 550

A dot placed after a note adds half the value of the note it follows:

## Dotted Half Note

$\dotminim$

$\frac{4}{4}$  2 + 1 = 3 Beats

## Dotted Quarter Note

$\dotcrotchet$

$\frac{4}{4}$  1 + ½ = 1½ Beats

---

### Prelude

A Prelude is a composition usually played before the worship service. It may be repeated all or in part depending on the time remaining prior to the service. More than one Prelude may be used.

---

# Prelude

GLOVER

**Dal Segno Al Fine - (D.S. al Fine)** Return to the sign ( 𝄋 ) and play to "Fine".

# All Hail The Power

EDWARD PERRONET - JOHN RIPPON

OLIVER HOLDEN

# Chords - I, V7

When three notes of a scale are played together, they are called a CHORD. When a melody is played with chords, harmony is created. You can add harmony to many familiar tunes with the use of only two or three chords. The two chords below will harmonize many tunes.

The first chord is called the I Chord. (C)

The second chord is called the V7 Chord. (G7)

The Roman Numerals indicate the degree of the scale upon which the chord is built. Chord symbols (letter names) are also given for further clarification. You will learn more about chords in this book and Level III of the David Carr Glover Piano Library.

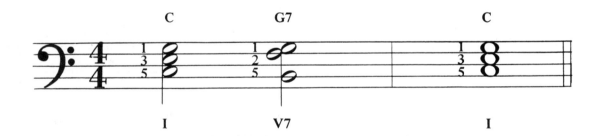

Most of the melodies in Level I of the David Carr Glover Piano Library were accompanied by double notes in the left hand. This was in preparation for the above chords.

Interlude is a short piece of music used during many worship services. Often times it is used at the close of hymns while the congregation is being seated or it is used during the time late worshipers are proceeding to their seats.

Andante

GLOVER - RICKER

# Half Steps And Whole Steps

**HALF STEP** — From one key to the next with no key in between.

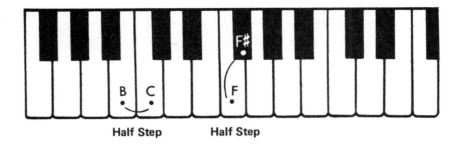

**WHOLE STEP** — From one key to the next with one key in between.

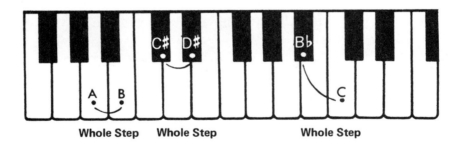

# Major Scale

**Play from Middle C to High C.**

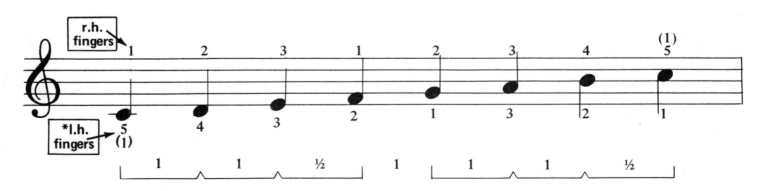

All Major Scales consist of 8 tones. They form a pattern of Whole Steps and Half Steps as shown above in the **C MAJOR SCALE.**

*Left hand can be played 8 keys lower (one octave).

**C** is another way to indicate $\frac{4}{4}$ meter signature.

It is called Common Time.

# Scaling In C Major

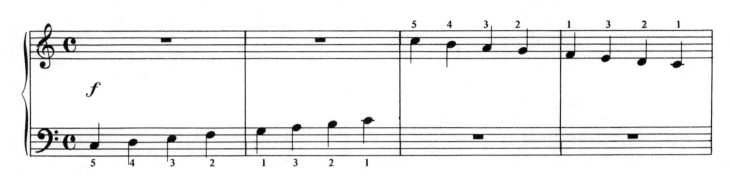

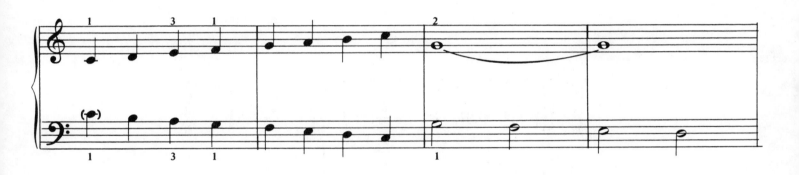

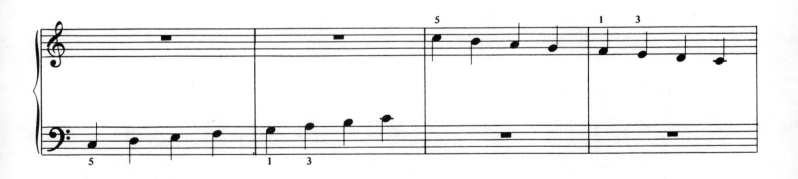

Adding one more chord to the two chords that you know, I and V7, will enable you to harmonize many more tunes.

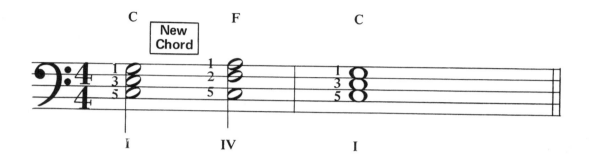

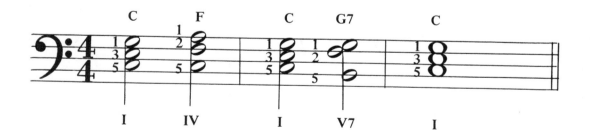

**TEACHER:**

For the student who has used Chords and Keys Level I as recommended on page 16 of the Church Musician Level I, Chords and Keys Level II could now be introduced. This book may also be used with Level III of the Church Musician.

PRISCILLA OWENS

WILLIAM J. KIRKPATRICK

*mf* We have heard the joy-ful sound! Je-sus saves! Je-sus saves! Spread the

tid - ings all a - round: Je-sus saves! Je-sus saves! Bear the

news to ev-'ry land, climb the steeps and cross the waves; On - ward!

'Tis our Lord's com-mand; Je-sus saves! Je-sus saves! A - men.

FDL 550

# Lighting Candles

RICKER

*You will learn more about Minor Chords later.

# G Major Scale - Key Signature F#

Left hand can be played 8 keys lower (one octave).

## Scaling In G Major

ELIZABETH P. PRENTISS

WILLIAM H. DOANE

*mf* More love to Thee O Christ, More love to Thee!

Hear thou the prayer I make on bend - ed knee;

This is my ear - nest plea: More love, O Christ, to Thee,

More love to Thee, More love to Thee! A - men.

# Chime Interlude

GLOVER

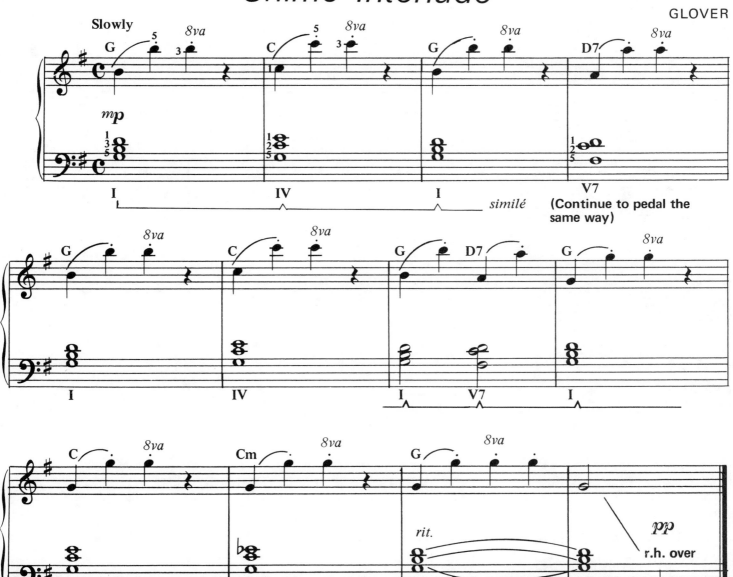

**\*You will learn more about Minor Chords later.**

# I Love Thy Kingdom Lord

TIMOTHY DWIGHT

AARON WILLIAMS

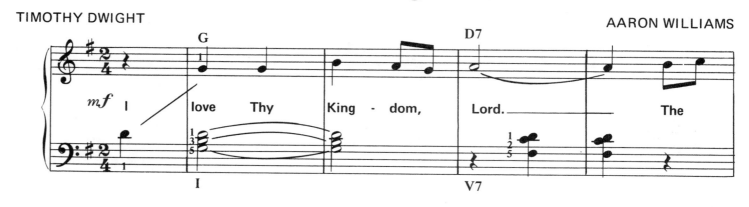

I love Thy King - dom, Lord. The

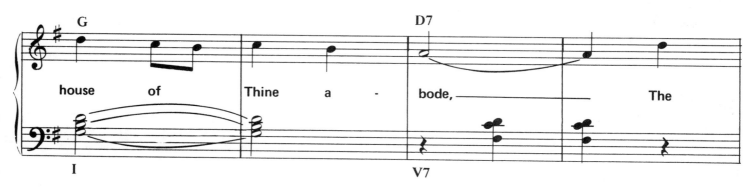

house of Thine a - bode, The

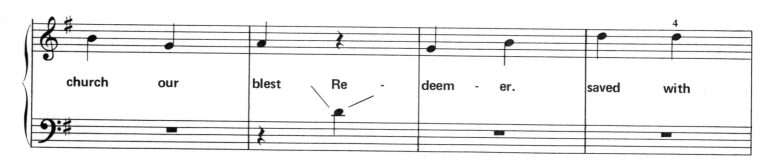

church our blest Re - deem - er. saved with

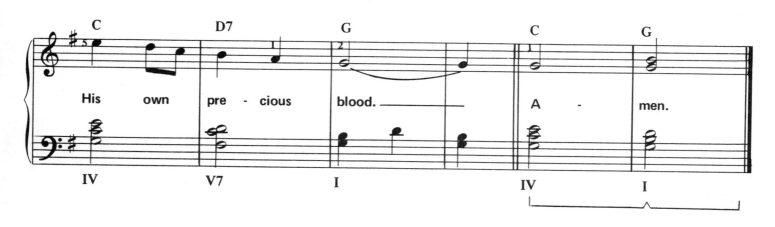

His own pre - cious blood. A - men.

# F Major Scale - Key Signature B♭

Left hand can be played 8 keys lower (one octave).

## Scaling In F Major

# Primary Chords In The Key Of F Major

# Stand Up, Stand Up For Jesus

GEORGE DUFFIELD

GEORGE WEBB

## Offertory

An Offertory is a composition played while the offering is being collected. It may be repeated all or in part depending on how much time is needed. It is usually played at a moderate speed and not too loud.

# *Offertory*

RICKER

Moderato

# Etude

## Other Ways To Play Etude

Fingering    Phrasing    Touch    Dynamics

# Fairest Lord Jesus
## Crusader's Hymn

RICHARD WILLIS

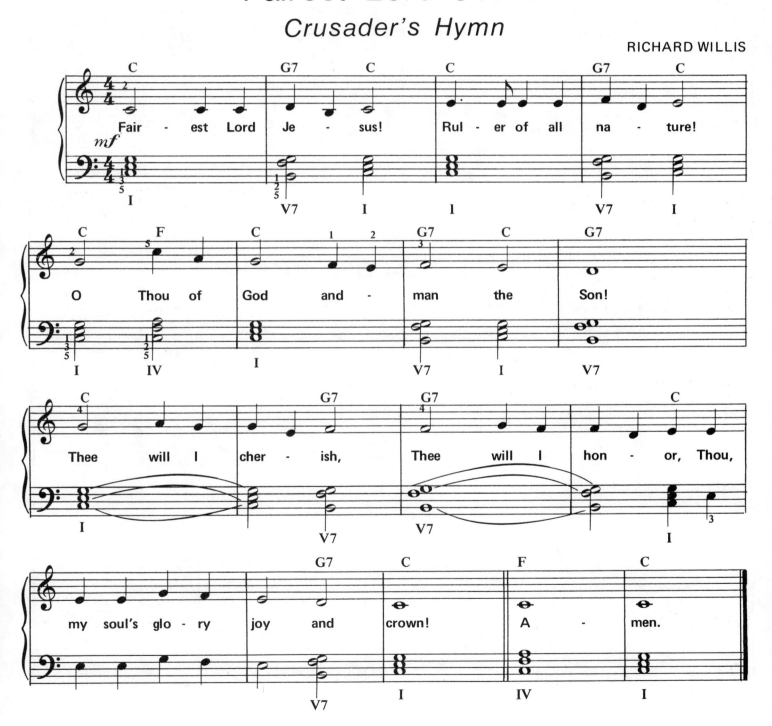

# G Major Scale Etude

# F Major Scale Etude

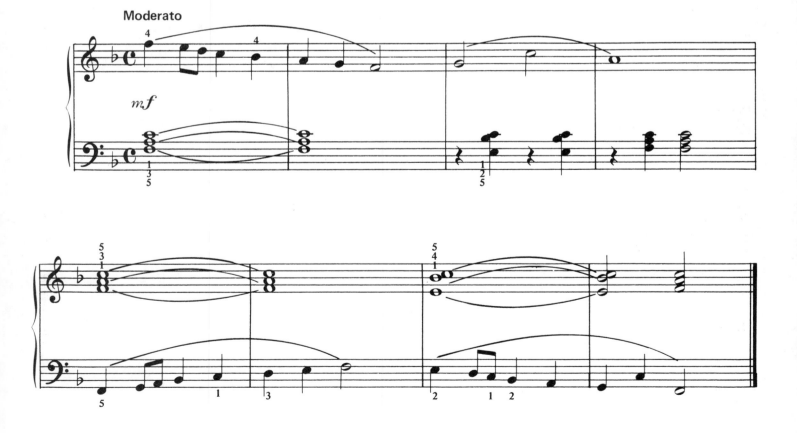

## Doxology

The Doxology is a composition expressing praise to God. In many churches it is played and sung after the offering.

# *Praise God, From Whom All Blessings Flow*
## Doxology

THOMAS KEN

G. FRANC

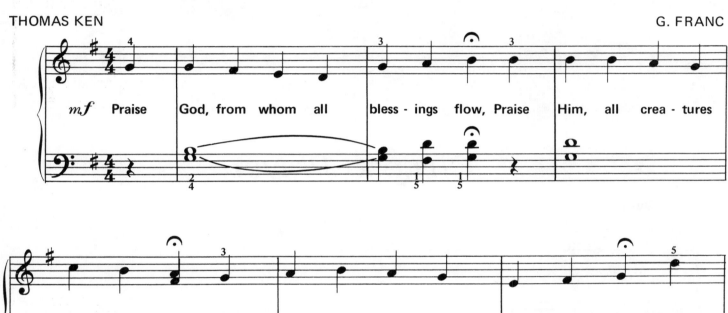

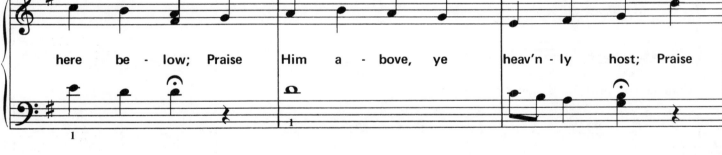

The Second Part to the Doxology found on page 26 of The Church Musician, Level I, may also be played with the above arrangement.

Chinese Prayer is recommended to be played for any special church occasion which may pertain to people of other lands.

# Chinese Prayer

GLOVER

Damper and Soft Pedal down throughout.

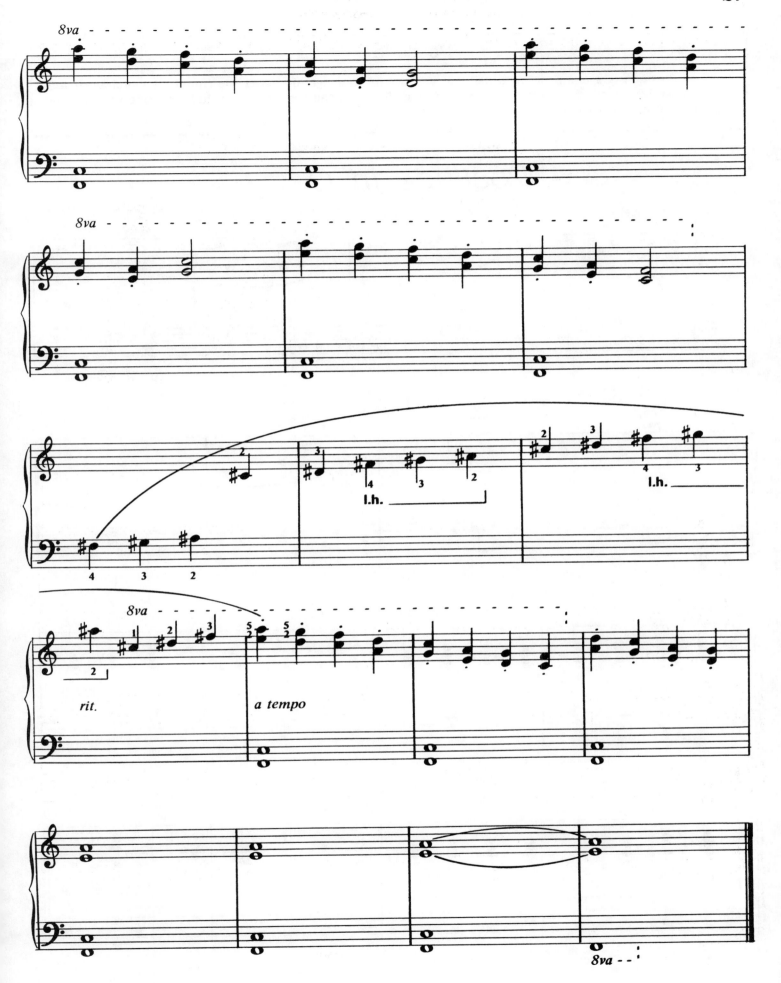

## Postlude

The Postlude is a composition usually played as the congregation leaves the church at the close of the worship service. If all the people have not left the church at the end of the Postlude, continue to play by repeating all or part of the piece.

# Postlude In C

RICKER - GLOVER

# Etude
## (Contrary Motion)

GLOVER

# Chord Prelude

GLOVER

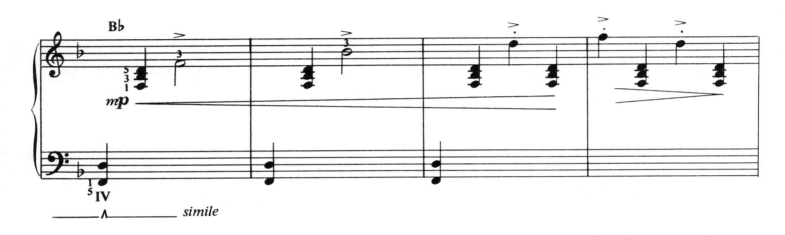

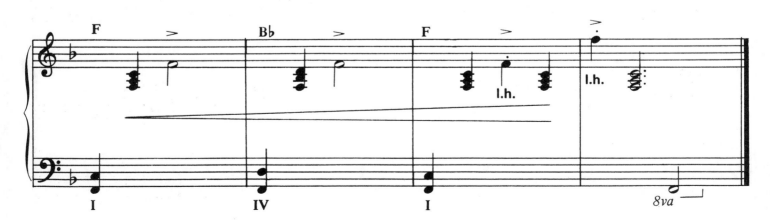

# A New Rhythm

## Six Eight Time or Meter Signature

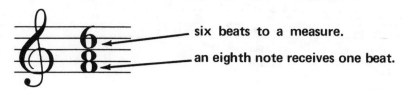

six beats to a measure.

an eighth note receives one beat.

| | NOTES | | BEATS | REST |
|---|---|---|---|---|

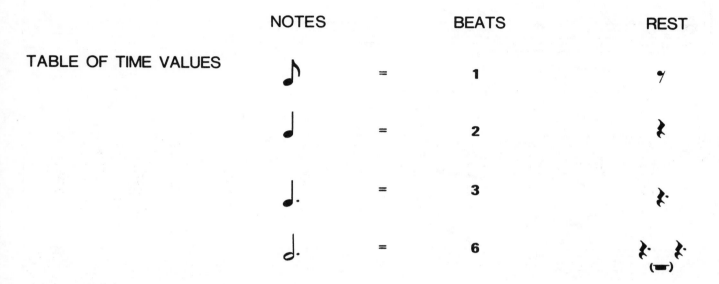

TABLE OF TIME VALUES

**CLAP and COUNT ALOUD several times —**

| 1 | 2 | 3 | 4 | 5 | 6 |
|---|---|---|---|---|---|
| SAY ——— Loud | soft | soft | Loud | soft | soft |

Ⓐ Moderato

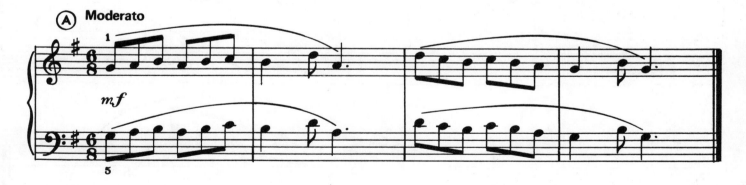

*mf*

Ⓑ Moderato

*mf*

FDL 550

# David's Harp

GLOVER - RICKER

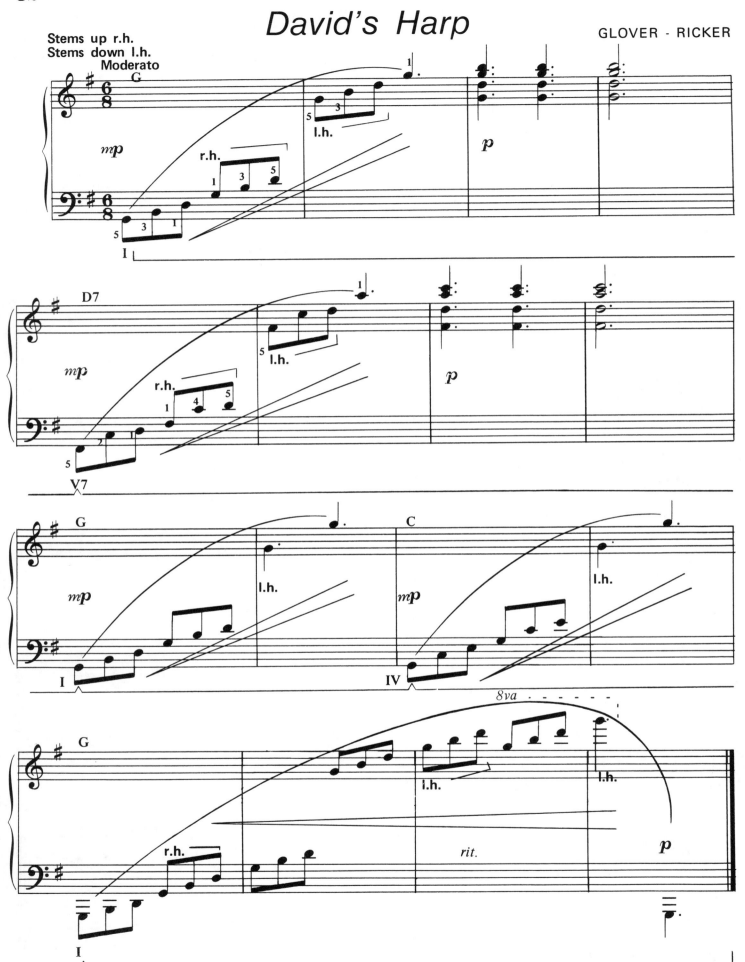

PHILIP P. BLISS

# D Major Scale - Key Signature F♯ C♯

Left hand can be played 8 keys lower (one octave).

## Scaling In D Major

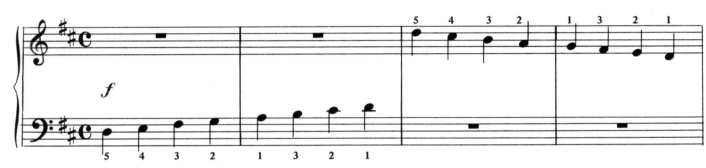

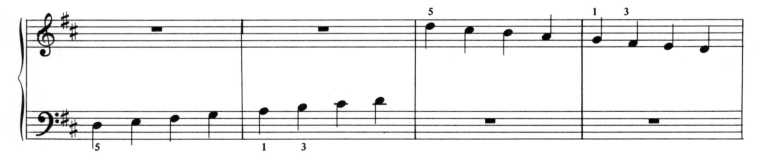

how the wind does blow! _____ It

stings the toes, and bites the nose, As

o - ver the ground we go. _____

*mp*

*dim.*

*8va*

FDL 550

# CHRISTMAS
## *Baby Jesus Lullaby*
### Treble First Part (Solo)

GLOVER

## *Baby Jesus Lullaby*
### (Bass Part)

*Baby Jesus Lullaby* **may be played as a solo, (omit Bass Player and Treble Second Player's Parts), as a duet, (use only one of the other two parts given), and as a trio (use all parts given). When played as a solo omit the first two measures of rest.**

# Certificate of Award

*This is to certify that*

_____

*has completed*

## The Church Musician Method
### Level Two

*of the*

**David Carr Glover**
**Christian Piano Library**

_____
DATE

_____
TEACHER